ARUNDEL
AND
THE ARUN VALLEY
IN OLD PHOTOGRAPHS

ARUNDEL
AND
THE ARUN VALLEY
IN OLD PHOTOGRAPHS

COLLECTED BY
JOHN GODFREY

ALAN SUTTON

Alan Sutton Publishing
Phoenix Mill · Far Thrupp · Stroud · Gloucestershire

First published 1990

British Library Cataloguing in Publication Data

Arundel & the Arun valley in old photographs
1. West Sussex. Arundel, history
I. Godfrey, John *1946–*
942.267

ISBN 0-86299-703-8

Typeset in 9/10 Korinna
Typesetting and origination by
Alan Sutton Publishing
Printed in Great Britain by
Dotesios Printers Limited

CONTENTS

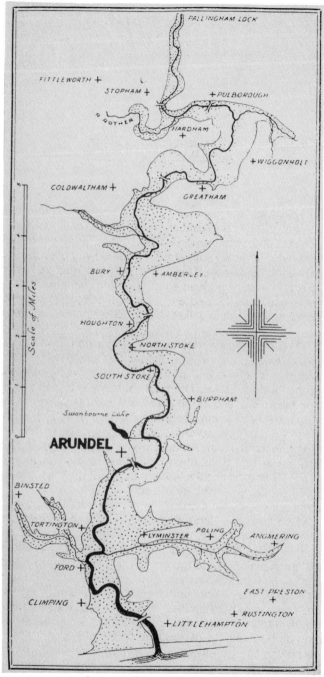

ARUNDEL AND THE ARUN VALLEY, from the *Sussex County Magazine*, 1930s.

INTRODUCTION

Sussex is like a block of Neapolitan ice-cream. It comprises three horizontal bands of colour: the pink of the clay Weald, the white of the chalk Downs, and the green of the fertile coastal plain. Superimposed on this background is the vertical pattern of the rivers draining the heavy soils of the Weald, carving gaps through the Downs and making their way to the sea. This pattern recurs across the county, the valleys of the Rivers Arun, Adur and Ouse sharing similar features. At the lowest point where the rivers could be bridged and where the topography provided naturally defensible positions, the great castle towns of Sussex grew up: Arundel, Bramber and Lewes.

Arundel is incomprehensible without an appreciation of its relationship with the Arun Valley, and vice versa. Arundel Castle was the seat of one of the most powerful families in England and most of the valley was – and still is – in the ownership of the Norfolk Estate. The Estate was the major employer in the area, not just on the farms but also in the town itself and the villages. Arundel was the market centre for the Arun Valley; the place where people came to buy and sell; to obtain goods and services not available in the villages and to take part in political activity and for recreation. From Arundel, the postmen set out on their bicycles to deliver the mail in the rural areas; the beers of the Arundel brewers were distributed to the village inns and the manufacturing industry of the town provided work and relative prosperity for large numbers of people.

The River Arun itself played a crucial role in this inter-relationship between the town and the valley. From earliest times, the river had been important as a communication route and as a means of transportation, particularly for heavy goods, in an area where the road system was notoriously inadequate. Like Lewes, Arundel lay at the junction of the two great rural economies of Sussex, the sheep and corn economy of the Downs and the cattle and woodland economy of the Weald. Timber from the Weald and lime from the Downland chalk pits were moved by river and coal and manufactured goods entered the area by coastal and river shipping, the two meeting at the port of Arundel, where extensive wharves and docks enabled large quantities of goods to be transferred and distributed.

Late nineteenth-century Sussex was, therefore, very different from the county today: Arundel was thriving as the economic centre of a prosperous agricultural estate, the castle itself and much of the town were rebuilt. Labour-intensive industry was well established in the town and, at Houghton Bridge, a major industrial settlement had developed to serve the Amberley Chalk Pits, at their peak the largest lime-burning works in Europe, employing over 100 men. In the countryside, the successful combination of sheep farming on the Downs and arable production in the lowlands required large numbers of skilled and unskilled labourers. The area was booming, self-confident and successful, with the castle town of Arundel as its natural focus.

It is the atmosphere of this period that this collection of photographs seeks to capture. Although many of the illustrations of rural life by George Garland, the Petworth photographer, were taken in the 1930s, the way of life they record is that of an earlier time which was already passing into history. The picture of life in Arundel and the Arun Valley presented in this collection relates primarily to the heyday of late Victorian and Edwardian England. The immense social and economic changes of the past 100 years have transformed the function of the area. Manufacturing, distribution and agriculture have been replaced by commuting, tourism, specialist retailing and capital-intensive agri-business. At the same time, alternative centres have developed and people in the villages now look further afield and to other towns for local services, rather than to Arundel.

But the striking fact is that these immense changes are not reflected in the physical appearance of the district. The boundary of the urban area of Arundel is much the same as it was 100 years ago and a visitor from the past would find that the look of the town has changed surprisingly little. Similarly, despite some expansion and change, many of the villages look much the same and, if the way the countryside is managed has altered – particularly as the result of the ploughing up of the Downs in the Second World War – the Arun Valley is still essentially an open, farmed landscape. What has caught my imagination in compiling this collection is this contrast between how things seem (which has changed relatively little) and how they really are (which has changed beyond belief). The reader who keeps this contrast in the forefront of his mind as he explores this collection will get the most out of this book.

This collection could not have been compiled without the help of a large number of kind people. In particular, I must thank Mrs Patricia Gill, the County Archivist, for allowing me to reproduce photographs in the care of the County Record Office, including the most important Garland collection; Mr Roy Huse, the County Librarian, for permission to use photographs in the West Sussex Library Service collection; the National Film Archive for permission to reproduce stills from the film *Tansy*, made at Burpham; Arundel Castle Trustees Ltd.; the Arundel Museum Society; the Trustees of the Chalk Pits Museum, Amberley; Apertures of Arundel; Beaver Photography; Mrs Winnie Burn; Mr W.J. Gordon; Miss Edith Haggett; Mr Roger Halls; Mr Oliver Hawkins; Mr Tom Hendrick; Mrs Janet Kelly; Mr Jack Lisher; Mrs Alison McCann; Mr David Nicholls of Selsey Photographic; Mr Gerry Nutbeem; Major J.A. Pearce; Mr Frank Penfold; Mr Nicholas Plumley; Mrs J. Duggan Rees; Mrs Sara Rodger; Mr Ken Rowsell; Mrs Iris Swaffield and Mrs Jean Tester.

Finally, I must thank Mr Martin Hayes, who helped me to identify important material in the County Library collection; Mr Kim Leslie, whose support in this and other enterprises has been quite invaluable; and my wife, Sally, whose detective work produced some of the best photographs in the book.

The Castle and the Park

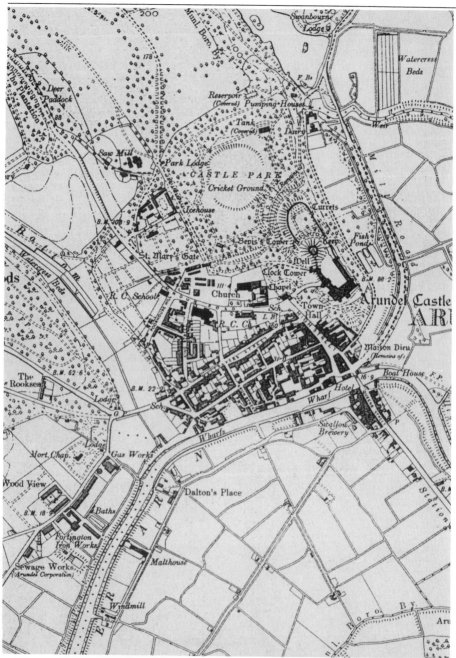

A MAP OF ARUNDEL reproduced from the Ordnance Survey 6 in Series, 1896. Note the absence of development to the west of the town, the Tortington Iron Works in Ford Road and the Swallow Brewery in Queen Street.

THE CASTLE FROM THE RIVER ARUN in the 1920s, showing landing stages and skiffs.

THE DRAWING ROOM OF ARUNDEL CASTLE furnished in Edwardian style, complete with aspidistras.

THE RECONSTRUCTION OF THE CASTLE, 1890–1903, resulted in the replacement of most of the work carried out early in the nineteenth century and the substitution, in a more correct style, of an entirely new west wing. The architect was C.A. Buckler.

To His Grace,

The Duke of Norfolk, Earl of Arundel, Earl Marshal and Hereditary Marshal of England.

We the workmen engaged in the restoration of your Castle of Arundel join heartily in the welcome offered to Your Grace to-day by the inhabitants of this Ancient Borough on the occasion of Your Grace's return with your Bride to your ancestral home. Our earnest hope and prayer is that both Your Grace, and Her Grace The Duchess, may long enjoy every blessing which health and happiness can bestow.

Signed on behalf of the Workmen.

George Kitt

March 5th 1904.

THE WORKMEN ENGAGED IN THE RECONSTRUCTION OF THE CASTLE welcome home Henry, 15th Duke of Norfolk, and his new bride in 1904.

MILL ROAD AND THE CASTLE, 1899. The new Mill Road was built by the 15th Duke of Norfolk in 1892 and lime trees were planted to create an avenue from the town to Swanbourne Lake. The Duke took two Arundel schoolchildren to ride in his carriage at the official opening of Mill Road.

THE PRESENTATION OF COLOURS to the 1st (Earl of Arundel's Own) and 2nd Arundel Boy Scout Troops, 16 July 1914. In the centre is the 15th Duke and his small son, later to be the 16th Duke, who wore a miniature scout uniform and presented each scout with a new scarlet silk scarf and a 5s. piece. Behind them: W. Haggett, F. Kendal (holding new colour), C. Coe and B. Treagus. Standing at the back are Captain G.S. Constable and Mr P.J. Dunworth, Scoutmasters.

A CRICKET MATCH IN ARUNDEL PARK, Littlehampton v. Arundel, c. 1890. Standing on the left, umpire Mr Charles 'Dodger' Bartlett, miller and sometime Mayor of Arundel. Players include members of the Constable and Beldam families, respectively brewers and lawyers of Arundel.

ARUNDEL PAGEANT IN THE CASTLE GROUNDS, 1923. This was one of many historical tableaux staged at Arundel Castle in the 1920s and '30s.

SWANBOURNE LAKE before the First World War. A view little changed today, except that the margins of the lake have been even further eroded by the feet of visitors and ducks.

AN EDWARDIAN MOTHER AND CHILDREN at Swanbourne Lake, c. 1902.

MISS EDITH HAGGETT takes the air with her brother in the park in the 1920s.

AN EARLY MOTOR CAR outside the High Street gate to the castle, 1920s.

CHURCH PARADE, 4th Royal Sussex Camp, Arundel Park, July 1912. In the background Hiorne's Tower, built in 1790 by Francis Hiorne, with flint and stone in chequer-board pattern as a model to demonstrate the architectural style he proposed to use for the first reconstruction of the castle.

A VIEW OF A SIMILAR PARADE in 1909, taken from Hiorne's Tower.

'FUN IN CAMP 1909', a more lighted-hearted view for soldiers to send to relatives and sweethearts. The Sussex and Surrey Yeomanry camped regularly in the park into the 1930s. During the Second World War Canadian troops were encamped in the park and were allowed to shoot the deer.

BERNARD, 16TH DUKE OF NORFOLK, addresses a British Legion rally in Arundel Park, July 1933.

LAVINIA, DUCHESS OF NORFOLK, presents a prize to William Shearman at Arundel Gymkhana, August 1937. Both these photographs are by George Garland, the Petworth photographer.

THE PRINCESS ROYAL INSPECTS SUSSEX RED CROSS VOLUNTEERS, Arundel Park, July 1938, two months before the Munich crisis.

A FOWLER 'GYROTILLER' with fuel trailer and living van at Park Farm, Arundel, 1934. The equipment was supplied by Penfolds, the Arundel agricultural engineers, who operated from the Tortington Iron Works in Ford Road. Frank Penfold stands centre, in nonchalant pose.

SECTION TWO

The Town

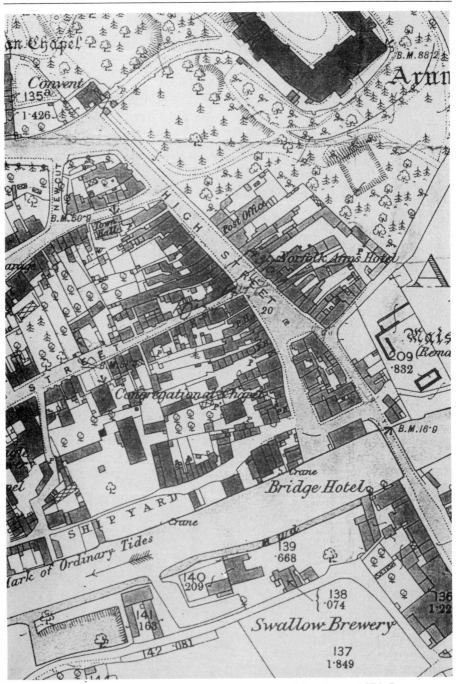

A MAP OF ARUNDEL reproduced from the Ordnance Survey 25 in Series, 1874–5.

MAY GOD PROTECT OUR NOBLE DUKE
IN THE HOUR OF DANGER
IS THE FERVENT WISH OF HIS EMPLOYEES

GOD SPEED TO HENRY, 15th Duke of Norfolk, off to the Boer War, 1899. This street decoration erected at the junction of London Road and The Cut to Maltravers Street nicely illustrates the economic and social relationship between the castle and the town.

THE HIGH STREET, late 1880s. On the left is the range of buildings that formerly housed the George Inn, the Norfolk Arms and Alfred Pain's ironmonger's shop under construction. Beyond was Atfield's Cement Mill at Portreeve's Acre, operated by Pepper's of Amberley and destroyed by fire in 1892. On the right, the home of Mr Charles Bartlett, miller and sometime mayor, which is now occupied by the Arundel Museum and Heritage Centre.

AN EARLIER VIEW OF THE SQUARE, with the Norfolk Arms on the right and the town pump, centre. The water supply was of variable quality and from time to time was blamed for outbreaks of typhoid in the town. Note the iron posts and chains in The Square which were used to form animal pens on market days. The posts may now be seen in Baker's Arms Hill and King's Arms Hill.

Arundel Market 50 years ago

THE MARKET IN THE SQUARE, 1880s. Formerly held in Maltravers Street (Old Market Street), the weekly cattle market was discontinued before the First World War. At one time, two markets were held each week, on Wednesdays and Saturdays. Note the premises of Watts and Nephew, drapers, on the left, next to the Red Lion, and, further up the High Street, the original offices of the *West Sussex Gazette*.

ANOTHER VIEW OF THE SQUARE in the early 1880s before the reconstruction of the buildings to the right of the Norfolk Arms.

ALFRED PAIN'S IRONMONGER'S SHOP has replaced the buildings adjoining the Norfolk Arms by 1900, leaving the original block containing Kimpton's fancy goods store and Lucas and Bowen's mineral water and ginger beer shop.

HORSE-DRAWN TRAFFIC IN THE SQUARE, 1906. Kimpton's has been replaced by the mock Tudor premises of the Capital and Counties Bank, now Lloyds Bank. Note the stone anvil on the gable of Alfred Pain's premises, symbolizing the ironmonger's trade carried on there. Note also the bunch of grapes on the Red Lion's inn sign, right, which survived through the reconstruction of the pub in the 1930s.

THE SQUARE in the 1920s, with early motor traffic.

THE SQUARE has traditionally been the scene of public and civic events in the life of the town. Here Duke Bernard and his new wife, Lavinia, are welcomed home by the townspeople after their wedding in 1937.

OTHER PUBLIC EVENTS FOR WHICH THE SQUARE WAS THE FOCUS included the celebration of Duke Bernard's coming of age and the annual carnival procession, here featuring the float of the Arundel Red Cross unit. The picture above shows the sweet shop kept by Mrs Kitty Cove, mother of Arundel's present Town Crier, Bill Beer. The duke's daughters always bought their sweets at Cove's.

THE OFFICES OF THE *WEST SUSSEX GAZETTE*, the county newspaper founded by William Woods Mitchell in 1853. Mitchell, far right in the picture, lived in Maltravers House and was Mayor of Arundel six times.

FOLLOWING A FIRE, the premises of the *West Sussex Gazette* were reconstructed and extended in the 1890s and new printing machines were installed. This picture, from the *Gazette*, shows the new Marinoni printing press in 1896.

THE INTERIOR OF ALFRED PAIN'S SHOP, c. 1900. The business still thrives today.

A MILITARY PARADE IN THE HIGH STREET to mark Queen Victoria's Diamond Jubilee, 1897. The Capital and Counties Bank on the right incorporated Arundel Old Bank, formerly run by Henty & Co. at Bank House, Town Quay.

THE NORFOLK HOTEL CARRIER, J.N. Hare, who plied between the Hotel and the railway station. Built in the 1780s, the Norfolk Arms is Arundel's premier hotel, with a fine assembly room on the first floor. With the coming of the motor car, the Hare family developed a successful garage business in premises behind the hotel.

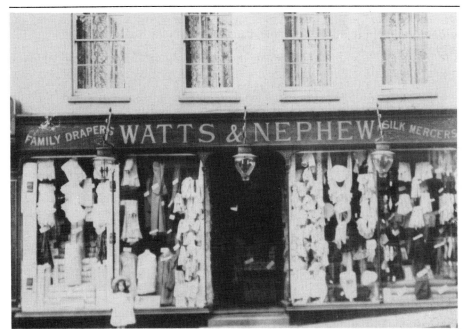

WATTS AND NEPHEW, DRAPERS, on the corner of Tarrant Street and the High Street. The shop was renowned for its pretty young lady assistants, many of whom married leading citizens and members of the Borough Council. It was here that Arundel writer and historian, Mr T.W. Hendrick, began his married life, renting seven rooms on the top floor for 10s. a week with electricity thrown in.

MR W.J. LASSETER, whose family operated the jeweller's business in The Square from the eighteenth century until the 1950s.

THE UPSTAIRS OF LASSETER'S SHOP before the First World War.

THE OLD CROWN INN BUILDINGS in The Square, occupied by Hammond, cycle agent, c. 1900. Hammond's was in business as a garage up until the Second World War and it was here that Mr T.W. Hendrick's three-wheeler Morgan was repaired after he did a double somersault in London Road in 1935.

THE SWAN HOTEL, which occupies a prominent corner site on the Town Quay and is well over 200 years old. The Swan was for a long time associated with the Constable family, who operated the Swallow Brewery in Queen Street, and with the Stevens family. Gordon Stevens was Mayor of Arundel more times than any other man. The Swan was well-placed beside both the market in The Square and the busy wharves of the port of Arundel.

ARUNDEL'S GRAND POST OFFICE, erected in 1892 in mock Tudor style when the 15th Duke of Norfolk was HM Postmaster General. The building is decorated in celebration of Queen Victoria's Diamond Jubilee in 1897. 'Skipper' Phillips was Postmaster of Arundel and Littlehampton for many years and refused offers of promotion to stay in Arundel. In times past a letter sent off early in the morning to the London office of the *West Sussex Gazette* received a reply on the same afternoon.

A VIEW OF ARUNDEL FROM THE TOWER OF THE SWALLOW BREWERY, Queen Street, in about 1870. This important photograph shows the 'old' Castle before the reconstruction of 1890–1903 and the Maison Dieu ruins intact prior to the building of Mill Road in 1892. The building in the foreground is the Bridge Hotel, pulled down in the 1930s, rebuilt in North Circular, Neasden style and now demolished. Centre, on the north bank of the river, is the Corn Store, used in later years as a chair factory.

THE RUINS OF THE MAISON DIEU, a medieval hospital or almshouse, in about 1885, before the construction of Mill Road and the new post office. Atfield's Cement Mill at Portreeve's Acre, in the distance, was built in 1861 and destroyed by fire in 1892.

ARUNDEL BOY SCOUTS take part in the celebrations to mark King George VI's coronation, 1936. 'Skipper' Phillips, Postmaster and Scoutmaster, stands on the left with arms folded.

BLACKMAN'S CONCERT PARTY, known as the Freeandeeses, a talented group of Arundel amateurs who entertained and amused local audiences for many years. Back row, from left to right: Clifford Coe, Madge Blackman (West), Dick Blackman (sen.), Frank Flavin. Front row, from left to right: Wally Booker, Dick Blackman (jun.), Margaret Horner, Geoff Blackman. Mr Dick Blackman was best known as a raconteur of Sussex humorous stories told in the authentic local dialect.

GEORGE ('GROGIE') BLACKMAN, the Freeandeeses' funny man, who subsequently became manager of the Gaiety Theatre in London's Aldwych.

THE NORTH-EASTERN END OF MALTRAVERS STREET, 1906, a favourite view for artists and photographers over the years. A perambulator stands outside No. 16, home of the Arundel historian and medical practitioner, Dr G.W. Eustace, whose *Arundel: Borough and Castle*, published in 1922, remains the standard history of the town. Note also the elegant young lady at No. 10 and the County Police Station, right, which moved to new premises in The Causeway in the early 1970s.

MOBILIZATION AT ARUNDEL, 5 August 1914. A view of troops parading in Maltravers Street. The building centre right housed the County Library for a number of years until it moved into the old school in 1975. The Sergeant in the front rank was an Ayling and his son, Ron, is the little boy watching, left. His father was killed in the first year of the war.

ANOTHER VIEW OF MOBILIZATION IN THE TOWN, taken on the same day. War had been declared on Germany at 11 p.m. on 4 August. The names of the many Arundel men who went away to war and did not return are recorded on the memorial in The Square, erected in 1922. Mr T.W. Hendrick understands that Arundel sent a higher percentage of its male population to the war than any other town in the United Kingdom.

MALTRAVERS STREET decorated for Queen Victoria's Diamond Jubilee celebrations, 1897. On the extreme right is Maltravers House, home of Mr William Woods Mitchell, founder of the *West Sussex Gazette*.

THE MITCHELL FAMILY AT HOME. Like many of the substantial houses on the south side of Maltravers Street, Maltravers House had extensive gardens running down to Tarrant Street and enjoyed views over open country.

OLD COTTAGES IN MALTRAVERS STREET, demolished in the 1890s when a new connection was made to the London Road. The two houses on the left, which still stand, were lived in for many years by members of the Tompkins family, agents to the Shelley family at Michelgrove, near Patching. Note the attractive street lamp on the corner.

MR AND MRS BERKSHIRE and subsequently Mrs Fanny Bishop (far right), a somewhat eccentric lady who died in the 1960s, occupied No. 14.

OLD COTTAGES IN TARRANT STREET, opposite what used to be the Co-operative Society premises, demolished c. 1900. Slaughter's grocer's shop is on the left. Mrs Slaughter was known locally as Nannie Weighfinger as the result of her unscrupulous trading practices.

JOHN BULL AND CO., BUTCHERS, in Tarrant Street, before the First World War. Arundel was particularly well served with butchers' shops and there seems to have been one on nearly every street corner — almost as many as the pubs! Today the only butcher's shop remaining is in The Square.

ABEL PIERCE, aged 81, wheelwright and blacksmith, at the forge which used to stand at the junction of Tarrant Street and Surrey Wharf. The business was founded in 1874 and closed in 1956. Abel used to turn up at the timber yard and sawmill in River Road looking for 'a little bit of crooked 'ard stuff for an hub'. He is shown here using a draw knife. Children would run across Tarrant Street from the Church of England School (now the County Library) to the smithy at the cry of 'Horse being shod!' to see what was going on.

THE OLD BRIDGE HOTEL IN QUEEN STREET and beyond, the Swallow Brewery and the premises of Messrs Daltons, builders. The licensee of the Bridge Hotel for a great many years was Mr Mustchen, who was also Company Secretary to the brewery. He was particularly proud of his glass-bottomed pewter tankards and once threatened Mr T.W. Hendrick and his friends with the police if any of them disappeared.

THE OLD WHITE HART, before its late Victorian reconstruction, and, left, Bridge House the premises of A. Herington and Son, drapers and outfitters.

THE HERINGTONS are a well-known Arundel family, supplying many of the town's mayors over the years. The family business in Queen Street closed in the early 1970s and the building is now a guest house.

A. HERINGTON & SON,

invite VISITORS to ARUNDEL to inspect their
WELL-ASSORTED STOCKS

OF

JUMPERS, COSTUMES, BLOUSES, MILLINERY,
DRESSES, GLOVES, AND HOSIERY.

CHILDREN'S & GENTLEMEN'S OUTFITTERS.

BOOTS & SHOES
of every description.

VALUES ARE ALWAYS THE KEENEST

AT

Bridge House, Arundel.

WORKERS AT DALTON'S, the builders in the 1880s. Dalton's premises were in Queen Street, on the site now occupied by the Circle K supermarket.

AN EARLY MOTOR CAR, possibly a Chevrolet, in Ford Road. The index letters BP were those of the old West Sussex motor taxation authority, whose functions were transferred to the National Vehicle and Driving Licensing Centre at Swansea in the 1970s.

A FOWLER PLOUGHING ENGINE in front of the newly built fitting shop at James Penfold's Tortington Iron Works, c. 1915. On the engine are Percy Penfold (centre) and 'Shucks' Arnold (driver). The works, one of Arundel's major employers, closed in 1988 and the site has been redeveloped with housing.

ARUNDEL FROM TORTON HILL shortly before the development of the area got under way.

THE OPENING OF ARUNDEL HOSPITAL, Chichester Road, by the Duchess of Norfolk, November 1931. The hospital, which replaced a Victorian building in King Street, is still very much in business today.

JAMES PENFOLD'S WALLIS AND STEEVENS EXPANSION ENGINE in the yard at Arundel railway station, 1904. John Henry Collins is on the wheel, Frederick Collins on tank.

THE CRAWLEY AND HORSHAM HUNT at Arundel railway station, 1931. The picture shows the extensive goods sidings, now a car park.

HOUSES AT THE TOP OF THE HIGH STREET. Sefton House, right, is a medieval timber-framed building. The house on the left, known as The Shambles, was demolished in the late nineteenth century and replaced by a mock Tudor building.

A MAYORAL PROCESSION BEFORE THE FIRST WORLD WAR. It remains the custom for the newly-elected mayor and members of the town council to process to church on 'Mayor's Sunday' in May. Sadly, the powers of the town council are now very limited.

ST NICHOLAS', Arundel's parish church in London Road. This view was painted when the road ran to the north of the church and before the expansion of the castle grounds in the 1890s. The chancel is the separate, Roman Catholic Fitzalan Chapel which has access only from the castle.

THE INTERIOR OF ST NICHOLAS' CHURCH, in the early twentieth century. The sanctuary has since been remodelled in accordance with current liturgical practice.

St. Philip Neri Church, Arundel

THE ROMAN CATHOLIC CATHEDRAL OF OUR LADY AND ST PHILIP HOWARD, built in 1870–3 by the 15th Duke of Norfolk as a potent symbol of Catholic emancipation. The architect was J.A. Hansom, who built Birmingham Town Hall and invented the Hansom cab. The church, which became the cathedral of the Arundel and Brighton Diocese in 1965, was originally dedicated to St Philip Neri, the patron saint of the Brompton Oratory.

MEN OF THE OLD ARUNDEL BOROUGH FIRE BRIGADE, in the late nineteenth century. Arundel at one time had two brigades: the duke's men operated in the castle and on the estate and the borough brigade looked after the town.

WELCOME HOME TO HENRY, 15th Duke of Norfolk and his bride, the former Hon. Gwendolin Constable-Maxwell, Baroness Herries, 1904.

BERNARD, 16THE DUKE OF NOR-FOLK, and his bride, the former Hon. Lavinia Strutt, arrive at Arundel railway station, February 1937. Following her husband's death in 1975, Lavinia, Duchess of Norfolk became Lord Lieutenant of West Sussex, the first woman ever to be appointed a Lord Lieutenant in England.

The Port and the River

A SKIFF ON THE RIVER, upstream of old Arundel bridge. The stone bridge was built in 1724, replacing a 1646 wooden bridge, and was itself replaced by the present bridge in 1935. Downstream is the busy port of Arundel, with warehouses and cranes in evidence.

AN EARLY PAINTING OF ARUNDEL BRIDGE with the Maison Dieu ruins to the right.

ARUNDEL BRIDGE, 1905. The view is dominated by the castle and the newly built post office, but also of interest are the Corn Store, left, the elegantly cantilevered walkways added to either side of the bridge in 1831, and Tom Buller's cottage to the right of the bridge. Note also the chickens on the Town Quay.

REBUILDING ARUNDEL BRIDGE, 1935, showing the construction of a coffer dam and a diver at work underwater. The construction of the dam resulted in the river being diverted under the Bridge Hotel. Its foundations were washed away and the hotel had to be demolished.

TOM BULLER'S COTTAGE, demolished in the 1930s. The Bullers have been associated with the river for generations and the present family run the Riverside Tea Gardens, from which boats may still be hired for expeditions up river.

SHIPS MOORED BELOW ARUNDEL BRIDGE, during the late nineteenth century.

COAL BEING DELIVERED TO ARUNDEL GASWORKS, Ford Road.

Arundel, View from Wharf.

TWO SHIPS DISCHARGING CARGO at the wharves below Arundel bridge. Arundel was a port and shipbuilding centre, with regular commercial traffic in the days before the development of the railways. Masted vessels were finally prevented from proceeding upstream to Arundel by the electrification of the railway line at Ford Bridge in 1930.

COAL BEING DISCHARGED at the wharf of the Arundel Co-operative Society, a site now occupied by the Tarrant Wharf housing development. Archaeological excavations before the houses were built revealed a Roman villa site but little information about the early history of the port of Arundel.

SHIPS WERE TOWED UPSTREAM FROM LITTLEHAMPTON by the steam tug *Jumna*.

A SAILING BARGE ON THE RIVER ARUN, in the late nineteenth century. The river was improved for navigation in the eighteenth century and between 1813 and 1816 the Wey and Arun Junction Canal was built to link Newbridge on the Arun to Shalford near Guildford on the River Wey. Thus the link with the River Thames was created, the canal being 23 miles long with 23 locks. By 1868 its role had been taken over by the railways and it was abandoned in 1871. This photograph shows sailing barge no. 64 with bargemaster Henry Doick and his sons Percy and Tom.

THE CORN STORE ON THE TOWN QUAY was destroyed by fire in July 1930.

THE FIRE, and the efforts of the fire brigade to bring it under control, attracted much interest and the events of the night of 12 July 1930 were captured on picture postcards.

The River,   Arundel.

THE RIVER TO THE SOUTH OF THE TOWN, a popular spot, then and now, for an afternoon stroll.

5371. ARUNDEL. - JUDGES LTD.

A VIEW taken from approximately the position of the present A27 road bridge.

GEORGE STEDMAN, BLACKSMITH, at his premises in River Road, c. 1905. The Stedmans are a long-established Arundel family, still very much in evidence in the town today.

GEORGE STEDMAN'S THREE CHILDREN. The younger boy, Ewart (right), in later life became a leading member of the Labour Party in the area. He died in 1989, aged ninety. The pushchair was made by George Stedman at the forge.

'GINGER' PARADINE drives a team of horses with a heavy load of timber to the premises of Arundel Timber and Sawmills Co. Ltd in River Road. Originally a shipyard, the timber business flourished in the nineteenth and early twentieth centuries. During the Boer War the yard won the contract for the supply of wooden tent pegs to the British Army.

THE WHARVES OF THE PORT OF ARUNDEL were lined with warehouses, some of brick and flint and some weather-boarded and tarred. Some survive and merit careful conservation but others, including this example in Arun Street, have been demolished.

ARUNDEL HAD AT LEAST TWO WINDMILLS ON THE RIVER: one upstream at Portreeve's Acre operated as a cement mill for much of the nineteenth century, and the other downstream at South Marshes (now Fitzalan Road). The latter survives, now converted into a house.

THE BLACK RABBIT INN, 1899. The inn was a favourite object of summertime expeditions, pleasure boats could be hired and a ferry operated across the river.

ARUNDEL REGATTA, 10 August 1910. This annual event was a feature of the Arundel social calendar until the First World War.

Burpham

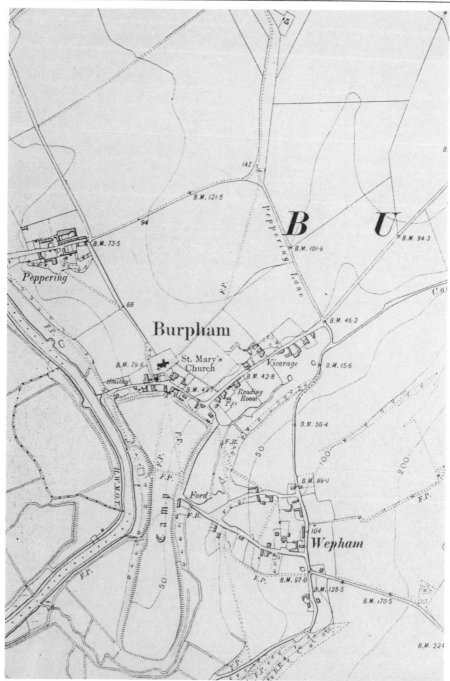

A MAP OF BURPHAM reproduced from the Ordnance Survey 6 in Series, 1909–10.

VIEWS OF BURPHAM AND THE ARUN VALLEY from a 1930s postcard. Burpham is three miles north of Arundel and derives its name from the Saxon *burh*, the fortified promontory overlooking the river which now contains the village cricket field.

AN OLD ENGRAVING of the river below the cliffs of the *burh* showing the ferry which provided access to the fields on the west bank of the river.

THE GEORGE AND DRAGON INN from the top of the tower of St Mary's parish church and the hamlet of Wepham, top left. Note the horse and cart outside the pub. On the right is Wall Cottage, part of Warre House (now Frith House), the home of the writer John Cowper Powys in the 1920s.

THE RIVER BANK AT BURPHAM, showing a camp site and evidence of the collection of reeds for thatching.

ANOTHER VIEW OF THE RIVER BANK, with Sunday afternoon strollers. The river at Burpham is now a backwater, the main flow being channelled through the Offham cut, built when the river was improved for navigation in the eighteenth century.

SHEPHERDS AND THEIR FLOCK on the road to Arundel. The Arun Valley was a good example of the traditional sheep and corn agricultural system of the Downs which lasted until the Second World War, when the drive for self-sufficiency resulted in the downland turf being ploughed up for arable production.

SHEEP DIPPING IN THE RIVER to clean the fleeces and wash out parasites. Note the men standing in barrels in the water in an attempt, probably futile, to keep dry.

MICHAEL BLANN, SHEPHERD, with his dog and flock on the Downs above Burpham. Blann was well-known for his singing and love of music and a collection of his songs has been published by Worthing Museum.

ANOTHER STUDY OF A DOWNLAND SHEP-HERD wearing the traditional smock made of heavy cotton, often oiled to keep out the worst of the weather.

THE POPULAR FILM *TANSY* was made in 1921 by the Hepworth Manufacturing Company partly on the Downs near Burpham. The film was based on a novel by the Revd Tickner Edwards, Vicar of Burpham from 1927 to 1935, and starred Alma Taylor as the shepherdess, Tansy.

ONE OF REVD TICKNER EDWARD'S MOST PRIZED POSSESSIONS was this photograph of himself with Alma Taylor, signed by the actress. It stood on the desk in his study for many years. In addition to his novels Edwards wrote on natural history and his book *The Lore of the Honey Bee* is a minor classic.

JAMES OLIVER, SHEPHERD TO THE COLLYERS OF PEPPERING FARM, lived in the cottage on the right in the 1930s with his family. His daughter, 'Girlie', was featured in the *Sussex County Magazine* in 1934: 'Gentle, unsophisticated and shy, she tends her father's flock on the scented downlands above Peppering High Barn'.

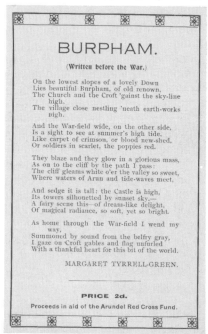

BURPHAM.

(Written before the War.)

On the lowest slopes of a lovely Down
Lies beautiful Burpham, of old renown,
The Church and the Croft 'gainst the sky-line
   high,
The village close nestling 'neath earth-works
   nigh.

And the War-field wide, on the other side,
Is a sight to see at summer's high tide,
Like carpet of crimson, or blood new-shed,
Or soldiers in scarlet, the poppies red.

They blaze and they glow in a glorious mass,
As on to the cliff by the path I pass:
The cliff gleams white o'er the valley so sweet,
Where waters of Arun and tide-waves meet.

And sedge it is tall: the Castle is high,
Its towers silhonetted by sunset sky.—
A fairy scene this—of dream-like delight,
Of magical radiance, so soft, yet so bright.

As home through the War-field I wend my
   way,
Summoned by sound from the belfry gray,
I gaze on Croft gables and flag unfurled
With a thankful heart for this bit of the world.

MARGARET TYRRELL-GREEN.

PRICE 2d.

Proceeds in aid of the Arundel Red Cross Fund.

A POEM ON BURPHAM BY MARGARET TYRRELL-GREEN sold in aid of the Arundel Red Cross Fund.

MR GOODYEAR, THE WHEELWRIGHT, and Mr Carpenter the postman, at the wheelwright's shop, Burpham, March 1933.

ROLLING CLOVER SEEDS at Burpham, 1920. A study by the Petworth photographer, George Garland, who regularly contributed pictures of agricultural subjects to the national press, including *The Farmer and Stockbreeder*.

THE INTERIOR OF ST JOHN'S PRIORY, POLING, which incorporates a Commandery of the Knights Hospitallers of St John of Jerusalem, founded in the twelfth century. The present house was largely built in 1830.

THE PARISH CHURCH OF ST MARY MAGDALENE, Lyminster, taken in the nineteenth century.

Slindon

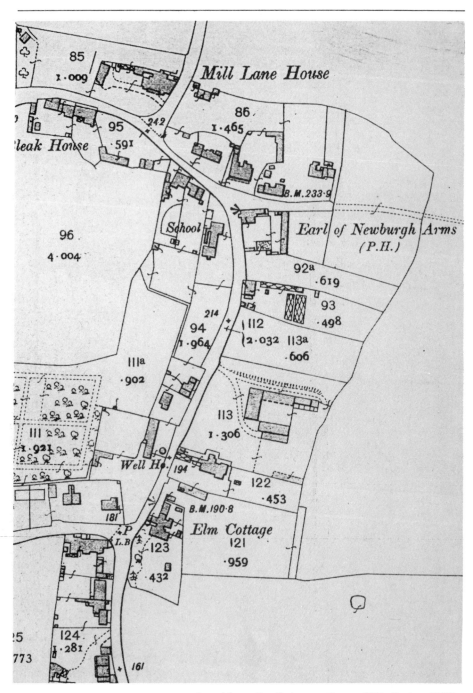

A MAP SHOWING PART OF SLINDON reproduced from the Ordnance Survey 25 in Series, 1910.

A STUDY BY GEORGE GARLAND, the Petworth photographer, of two aged inhabitants of Slindon at the lime tree near the parish church, 1935.

MR BURCH AT DAIRY COTTAGE, probably at the time of Queen Victoria's Diamond Jubilee, 1897. The cottage bears the date 1749 and takes its name from the fact that the building behind was for many years a dairy, supplying cream and butter to Slindon House.

MARTIN'S FORGE IN DYERS LANE, c. 1850, showing Mr Bateman shoeing a horse. The present forge is next to the Coronation Hall. Built to replace Martin's forge soon after this photograph was taken, Slindon forge is still very much in business.

SLINDON POND BEFORE THE FIRST WORLD WAR. The Grange on the left was once the home of Hilaire Belloc and his mother. Right, the vicarage, home of the Revd William Chantler Izard and his second son, the Revd Arthur Izard, who were rectors of Slindon from 1865 to 1919.

WELL NAP CORNER in the nineteenth century, Manchester House and the village stores are on the left.

THE RUINS OF THE DOG AND PARTRIDGE, an old inn on Slindon Common with smuggling connections. It was here, on a dark night in 1749, that the smuggler Richard Hawkins was whipped to death for cheating his comrades. His body was dumped in the pond at Parham Park.

THE FORMER SLINDON CHURCH OF ENGLAND SCHOOL, left, built by the Revd Chantler Izard in 1871. The school is now a private house and has been replaced by a modern building opposite the Coronation Hall. Ahead is the Newburgh Arms, the headquarters of the famous Slindon Cricket Club, named after the Earls of Newburgh, lords of the manor of Slindon.

AN EDWARDIAN SUNDAY SCHOOL OUTING leaving the lime tree near the parish church. The steam engine and wagons belonged to farmer Charles Bowley of Gumber, Court Hill and Garston Farms. Note the separate wagons for adults, girls and boys.

A SLINDON HORSE BUS before the First World War. In the early 1900s members of the Palmer family ran a two horse bus daily, to and from Barnham station. This photograph shows Harry Palmer driving and among the passengers are Thomas Burch and Bert Dean, who was killed in the First World War.

AFTER THE FIRST WORLD WAR, the horse-drawn bus was replaced by a converted field ambulance and then by a purpose-built motor bus, The Silver Queen, which provided an essential service for Slindon people for many years. The bus was run by Mr Cecil Walling, shown here with his wife and Mr Ernest Parker.

SLINDON HOUSE, 1927. Now a boys' school, Slindon House is on the site of what was originally a palace of the Archbishops of Canterbury. Substantially rebuilt in 1921, the house and the surrounding 3,600 acre estate were given by Mr Wooton Isaacson to the National Trust in 1948.

THE STAFF AT SLINDON HOUSE, 1880, in the days of the Newburghs.

SLINDON HOUSE before its reconstruction.

THE GREAT HALL, Slindon House, a photograph by George Garland which appeared in the *Sussex County Magazine* volume 427.

SLINDON BAND OF HOPE, 1890. The Band of Hope Union of children's temperance societies was founded in 1855 to discourage young people from drinking alcohol.

SLINDON BRASS BAND, 1870.

TEA GARDENS. Large and Small Parties Catered for.

Good Accommodation for Motorists,
—— Cyclists, and Visitors. ——

Approved and Recommended by
Cyclist Touring Club and Royal
National Cyclist Union.

MOTOR GARAGE.

NEWBURGH ARMS, SLINDON, SUSSEX

GOOD STABLING.

Wines, Spirits, and Beers
— of the finest quality.—

Good Bus Service to Surrounding Towns.

Proprietor - - - GEORGE EVANS.

THE NEWBURGH ARMS, the one pub left in the village today, was offering facilities for cyclists and motor tourists in this 1920s advertisement.

SLINDON CRICKET CLUB, 1914. Richard Newland, 'the father of cricket', lived and died in Slindon and, in 1744, captained an England XI which was virtually the Slindon team. Not without cause was Slindon known as 'the cradle of English cricket'. This photograph includes members of the Bowley family and also Arthur Dean (back row, second left) and the team's mascot, Jimmy Dean, handyman at Slindon House (seated on grass, right). Jimmy wrote 'Slindon Notes' for the *West Sussex Gazette* for forty years and kept a number of records and diaries.

SLINDON CRICKET CLUB, 1923. Jimmy Dean (now with one leg) standing, second right; Mr Evans, the landlord of the Newburgh Arms standing on Jimmy's left and Mr Wooton Isaacson of Slindon House seated centre with hat and cane. The club celebrated its 250th anniversary in 1981 with a match against celebrities from the Chichester Festival Theatre.

THE SPUR HOTEL in the 1930s, originally the George Thomas Arms, named after the owner of Dale Park, Madehurst. The Spur was owned by Henty and Constable, the Chichester and Arundel brewers. The home of the Henty family was at Avisford Park.

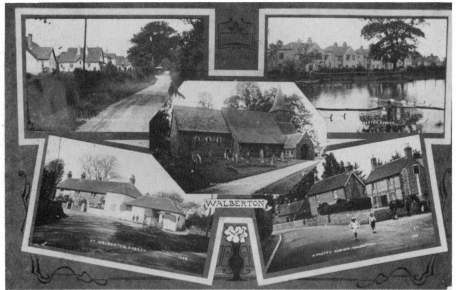

A POSTCARD SHOWING VIEWS OF WALBERTON, the village south of Slindon Common and the Arundel–Chichester road in the 1930s.

EDWARDIAN VIEWS of Walberton Green and the Village Hall, Walberton.

Walberton. The Village Hall.

SCHOOLCHILDREN DRINKING MILK AT BIDDLESIDE FARM DAIRY, Slindon, April 1935. A study by George Garland. *The Story of Slindon*, compiled by Slindon Church of England School and Slindon Young Farmers' Club soon after the Second World War and now in the County Record Office, records that, at that time, Biddleside Farm, a dairy farm of 220 acres, was worked by Mr Thornton, the farmer; a manager and three labourers; three 'repatriated Germans' and two Land Girls, Rose and Edna.

Bury and Bignor

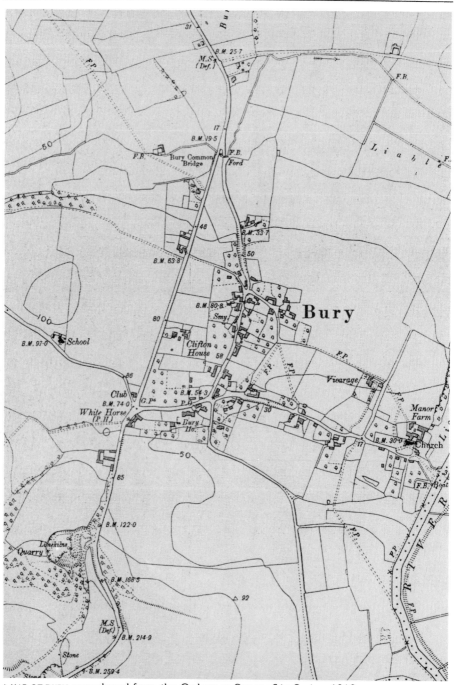

A MAP OF BURY reproduced from the Ordnance Survey 6 in Series, 1910.

THE FERRY ACROSS THE RIVER ARUN AT BURY, 1902. The ferry, kept for many years by a Mrs Shepherd, was a popular way of getting from Bury to Amberley, avoiding a four mile journey via Houghton Bridge.

A LATER VIEW OF THE FERRY, looking east to Amberley Chalk Pits, 1931. From 1927 to 1955 the ferry was kept by Mr Bob Dudden, known as the last of the ferryman or, more colourfully, the last of the harbour-masters. A former naval man, Bob attended Bury Church of England School where he met his future wife, Minnie.

BUILDING A BONFIRE ON BURY HILL to celebrate the 16th Duke of Norfolk's coming of age, 1929.

THE WHITE HORSE AND COTTAGES at the bottom of Bury Hill, early 1900s. One of the cottages on the left was the home of Charles Kilhams, a farm labourer who worked on Bury Manor Farm from the age of seven in 1861 until he died in 1939, aged eighty-five (see p. 113).

THE VILLAGE STREET, BURY. Much information about Bury in former times is included in *Within Living Memory*, a book of village life compiled by members of the Bury and West Burton Women's Institute in 1958 and now in the County Record Office.

AN RAC SCOUT AT BURY GATE, May 1933. Note the advertising hoardings, including one relating to new houses for sale on the Bay Estate, Aldwick.

TAKING THE COWS TO MILKING, Bury, June 1932.

HAY MAKING AT BURY, June 1932, the Downs and the Amberley Chalk Pits are in the distance.

GIRLS HELPING WITH FARMWORK at Bury, 1931, with a car pulling a hay-rake. George Garland's photographs of girls in the countryside were carefully posed and often included his wife, Sally, who helped him to run the Petworth business.

CHARLES KILHAMS (see p. 109), broadcasting seed by hand from a 'sidlup' (seed-lip) at Bury, 1932. He was a popular local character and was much photographed in later years. When interviewed in 1936, Charles told the reporter: 'There's hardly a villager in the village today. These "two-house gents" have pushed them out and you can't get a house for love nor money.' Clearly, the problem of affordable housing in Sussex villages for local people is not a new one!

HORSE AND CART at West Burton, October 1933.

BURY FOOTBALL TEAM, March 1936, on the occasion of the local derby with the West Burton team.

RE-THATCHING THE OLD SHOP, Bignor, February 1935. The Old Shop, a fifteenth-century half-timbered cottage with a first-floor jetty and wooden spandrels in front of a recessed centre, has always been a favourite subject for artists and photographers (including George Garland).

THRESHING AT BIGNOR, August 1948. Farmer Henry Tupper standing by the smoke-box of the Burrell traction engine belonging to James Penfold Ltd of Arundel with a Clayton and Shuttleworth threshing machine.

MAY DAY CELEBRATIONS at Sutton, May 1936.

A GRAVEDIGGER in Sutton churchyard, 1931.

SUTTON VILLAGE STORES, 1931. The young lady advertising Carter's seeds naturally attracted George Garland's attention. The shop is now closed and the building is a private house.

SECTION SEVEN
Amberley

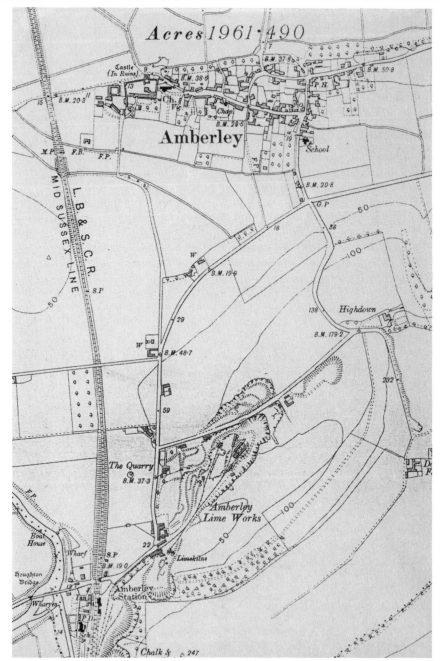

A MAP OF AMBERLEY reproduced from the Ordnance Survey 6 in Series, 1910.

AN AMBERLEY VILLAGE COUNCIL MEETING outside the Black Horse: an early and well-known study which includes members of many families whose names were familiar in the village for many years, including Searles, Ruffs, Hooks, Scutts and Fields.

AMBERLEY CHURCH AND CASTLE, 1906, with the horsepond in the foreground. Amberley Castle was built by the Bishops of Chichester and was visited by King Charles II on his flight to France after the Battle of Worcester. The castle was for many years the home of the Emmett family and is now a hotel and restaurant.

'POP' COOTER OUTSIDE HIS BAKERY in Church Street, photographed by George Garland, February 1935.

GRANNY PHILBY, great-grandmother of members of the Hook family still living in the village.

A LEE BABY, Amberley, July 1934. The Lees and the Strudwicks were, and still are, well-known farming families in the village. The Strudwicks now farm at Downs Farm, above the Chalk Pits.

AMBERLEY BRASS BAND, 1904. The players included Charlie Hammond, Bob, Jack and Fred Philby, Dave and Harry Dinnage, Harry Smith and Harry West.

AMBERLEY MAY REVELS, 1929, with the procession in School Road. Stream Cottage is on the left, The Laurels ahead.

Church Street, Amberley

CHURCH STREET. Members of the well-known Amberley family, the Lees, still live in the third house on the left.

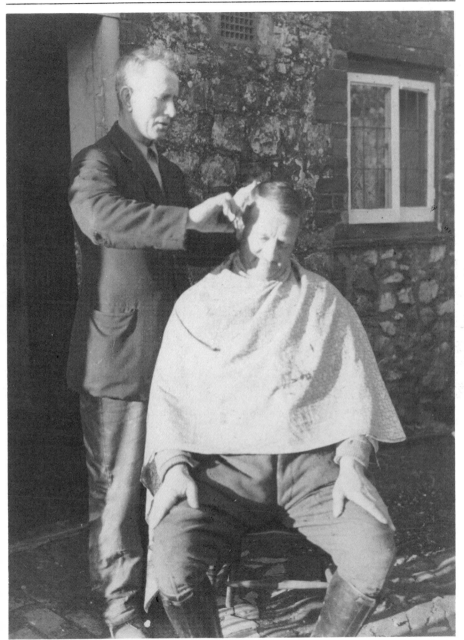

THE VILLAGE BARBER: Bert Hook cutting Riley Baker's hair. Bert worked full-time in the Chalk Pits, having started off as a groom to the Pepper family, and supplemented his income by cutting hair. He cycled round the local villages visiting customers and charged 6d. and a glass of cider.

FILMING IN HOG LANE, July 1932. The film was *The Man from Toronto*, directed by Sinclair Hill, starring Jessie Matthews and Sam Hunter. The event caused great excitement in the village.

A FREAK DOUBLE-HEADED CALF at Amberley, August 1932.

HARVESTING OATS at Amberley, August 1932.

THE WHARF AT HOUGHTON BRIDGE in about 1905, now occupied by a caravan site. Coal for firing the lime kilns at Pepper's works was brought upstream by barge and the finished lime was then taken away by water. The use of the river continued long after the coming of the railway in 1863.

LIME HAS BEEN BURNT AT AMBERLEY SINCE THE MIDDLE AGES but by the 1870s production became organized on an industrial basis under the management of the Pepper family. Up to 100 people worked in the Chalk Pits and, at its peak, the works was one of the largest of its type in Europe, lime being used for building purposes (before the introduction of Portland cement) and as a fertilizer. The lower picture shows the characteristic three-wheeled 'Dobbin' carts used in the pits. Taken in the early 1900s.

WORKERS AT THE FACE AND OUTSIDE THE COMPANY OFFICES, probably on pay day.

THOMAS CUNNINGHAM PEPPER, founder of the firm, with his grandson, Hugh Thomas John Cunningham Pepper, in the grounds of Quarry House, c. 1910.

SKIFFS FOR HIRE downstream of Houghton Bridge in the 1930s. Houghton Bridge grew as an industrial settlement serving the Pepper works, but was always a popular spot for excursions, boating and fishing.

A FOOTBALL TEAM OUTSIDE THE CRICKETERS AT HOUGHTON BRIDGE. The pub closed when Peppers' works in the Chalk Pits across the road was run down and it is now a private house.

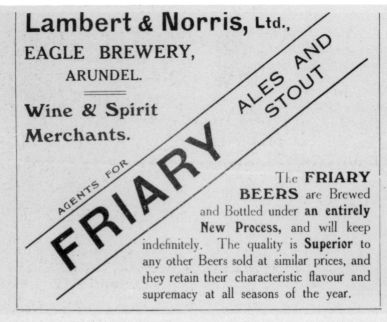

LAMBERT AND NORRIS operated the Eagle Brewery in Tarrant Street, Arundel and had a number of tied houses in the surrounding villages including Houghton Bridge.

A GROUP OUTSIDE THE HOUGHTON BRIDGE HOTEL, in the 1920s.

HENTY & CONSTABLE
(BREWERS), Ltd.

Manufacturers of the celebrated

SUSSEX ALES AND STOUT.

WINE & SPIRIT MERCHANTS

And Makers of High-Class

MINERAL AND AERATED WATERS.

BRANCH OFFICE :
SWALLOW BREWERY,
Tel. 99. **ARUNDEL.**

HEAD OFFICE :
WESTGATE BREWERY,
CHICHESTER.

Branches also at Littlehampton and Worthing.

THE HOTEL WAS OWNED BY HENTY AND CONSTABLE, whose Arundel offices were at the Swallow Brewery, Queen Street.

MEMBERS OF HOUGHTON BRIDGE AND DISTRICT ANGLING CLUB at the Houghton Bridge Hotel, 1927.

AMBERLEY STATION, 1962. Extensive sidings served the Chalk Pits and, in the goods yard, the old Southern Railway provided camping coaches for holiday-makers. From 1894 to 1968, the booking office doubled as a post office and Mr Jack Lisher is seen here issuing a family allowance and a day return to Littlehampton.

THRESHING TACKLE, belonging to James Penfold Ltd. of Arundel, outside the George and Dragon, Houghton, August 1935. Houghton House is on the right. The driver and his mate are inside the pub.

HARROWING AT RACKHAM, 1932, the old village school is on the right. The pinewoods on the ridge were badly damaged in the storm of October 1987.

WOMEN AND CHILD outside a cottage in South Lane, Houghton, in the late nineteenth century.

ALMOST THE SAME SPOT in the 1930s. Sally Garland is the solitary figure walking down the lane with her bicycle and water container, an example of Garland's 'hiking girls' genre (see pages 146–147).

BLUEBELL PICKING at Parham, May 1928.

PARHAM CRICKET TEAM, June 1936.

The Wildbrooks

THE WATER MEADOWS known as the Amberley Wildbrooks extend from Amberley to Pulborough. The Wildbrooks were traditionally subject to winter flooding and, despite some flood prevention measures over the years, still are today. The Wildbrooks provide an unusual and very important natural habitat and are now protected as a Site of Special Scientific Interest.

A SECOND STUDY OF THE AMBERLEY WILDBROOKS IN WINTER. Both these photographs are by Major J.A. Pearce of Westergate and show the open, flat landscape of the Arun Valley.

EARLY POSTCARD VIEWS OF WATERSFIELD, on the western edge of the Wildbrooks, by Searle, the local photographer.

CRICKET AT WATERSFIELD, May 1933. The Sussex County team played here from time to time in the 1930s, appreciating the charm and tranquillity of this essentially English scene.

LONDON ROAD, COLDWALTHAM, before the construction of the bypass which took the heavy traffic out of the village. The Labouring Man is on the left.

A TENNIS PARTY AT COLDWALTHAM, March 1927. George Garland is third from left, back row, strumming his racquet like a banjo.

A GROUP OF GARLAND HIKING GIRLS on the River Arun, August 1931. Sally Garland is in the centre.

GARLAND GIRLS AGAIN, this group at Quell Farm, Greatham, 1932. These hiking photographs, all carefully posed with appropriate props and featuring Sally Garland and her friends, became a speciality in the 1930s.

WILFRID MEYNELL, the patriarch of a literary and artistic family community at Humphrey's, Greatham, in the 1930s. Wilfrid and his wife Alice wrote here and while living at Greatham as their guest, D.H. Lawrence wrote *The Rainbow*.

Pulborough and Fittleworth

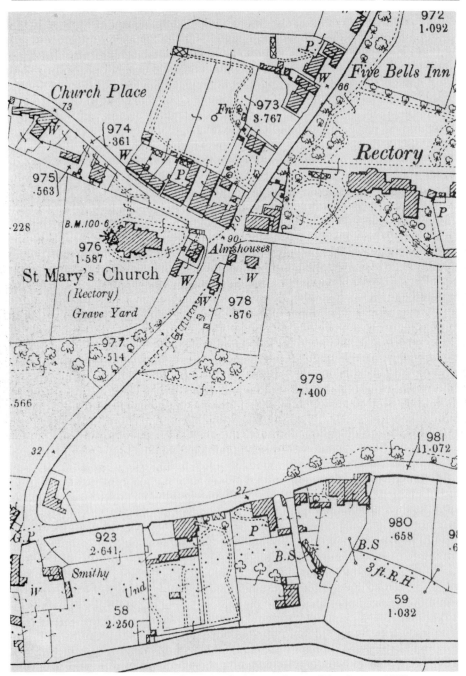

A MAP OF PULBOROUGH reproduced from the Ordnance Survey 25 in Series, 1895.

SWAN BRIDGE, PULBOROUGH, 1914, the Swan Hotel and Garage are in the centre.

SWAN CORNER in the 1930s, the Swan Hotel left and, right, the premises of F.J. Orford, saddler and harness maker.

MR F.J. ORFORD, in his shop, July 1935.

PULBOROUGH RAILWAY STATION, 1925. The smart turnout of the two men, particularly the gleaming boots, suggest a carefully posed photograph rather than a spontaneous snap.

TWO VIEWS OF PULBOROUGH MARKET, 1936. The upper picture shows the auctioneer Newland Tompkins and the lower a well-known Jewish market trader, described by S.P.B. Mais as 'a silver-tongued persuader'.

STOPHAM BRIDGE with Garland girls and the new traffic lights, the first to be installed in West Sussex, taken in the mid-1930s.

THE INTERIOR OF THE WHITE HART, STOPHAM, January 1936. Mr Blunden, the landlord, is seated second from the right and his wife on the left.

THE SWAN HOTEL, FITTLEWORTH, 1914, with the famous inn sign high above the road. Fittleworth was a favourite destination for cyclists and was also popular with fishermen.

ARTISTS WERE ALSO ATTRACTED TO THE VILLAGE, with its river, mill and pretty cottages, an association reflected in the Picture Room, a feature of The Swan for many years. This photograph was taken in 1914.

FITTLEWORTH MILL, 1906. Fittleworth lies on the River Rother, which joins the River Arun at Pulborough. The river was improved for navigation in 1794 by the 3rd Earl of Egremont, linking Midhurst and Petworth with the Arun Navigation.

FITTLEWORTH SMITHY, October 1933. A favourite Garland subject, the smithy was run by the Parfoot brothers.

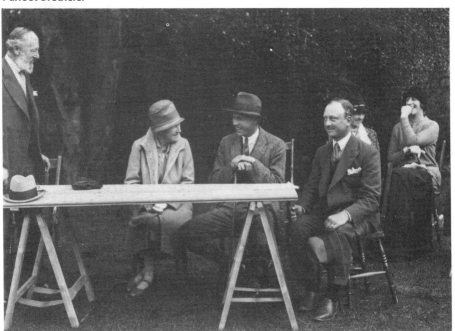

FITTLEWORTH RIFLE CLUB, June 1935, waiting for the presentation of prizes.

PULBOROUGH FATSTOCK SHOW, 1931.

PICTURE CREDITS

THE YOUNG ARTIST, EVERARD MEYNELL, later of Greatham, 1904.